I PREDICT
1986

A Year
Of World
Destiny

LESTER SUMRALL

Unless otherwise indicated
all Scripture quotations are taken from
the *King James Version of the Bible*.

I PREDICT 1986
ISBN 0-937580-45-7
Copyright © 1985 by Lester Sumrall
Published by LeSEA Publishing Company
P.O. Box 12
South Bend, Indiana 46624

CONTENTS

INTRODUCTION

I PREDICT THE YEAR OF 1986
TO BE A YEAR OF DESTINY

I am in love with the twentieth century.
It was young, in its teens, when I made
    my entry.
Only the 20th century have I known.
In succeeding decades by all waters
    have I sown.

The teens of the 20th century was the
    decade of my birth.

World War I was ready to shake
   planet Earth.
The twenties I knew because I began
   to preach;
Rural areas, towns and cities I did reach.

The thirties were great—I became
   a missionary!
To some friends I had become
   a reactionary.
In the forties I was married and
   happy as could be.
The fifties saw the growth of
   a family tree.

In the sixties our ministry spread to
   many lands,
The seventies revealed the fulfilling
   of the divine plan.
The eighties gave me television
   by satellite
To reveal God's power and might.

The mid-eighties added worldwide
   shortwave;

A billion souls could learn of Jesus'
    power to save.
Now Century Twenty-one belongs to
    the Christ of God;
He will have defeated His enemies at
    Gog and Magog.

For a millennium of years He shall
    over this earth reign—
It will be a thousand years of rule
    without a stain.

Year Of Joy

In the memorial year of 1986
The real and the unreal shall surely
    not mix.
Jesus' followers shall victoriously
    do the right,
Worshiping their living Lord with all
    their might.

Some shall come before Him joyfully
    dancing;
The people of unbelief will say they
    are prancing.

Others will clap their hands for sheer joy:
The father, the mother, the girl, the boy!

Year Of Hurts And Tears

For some the calendar year of 1986
    will be a time of deep hurt.
Those who listen to evil will be ground
    into the dirt.
When, if they turn their hearts toward
    the sky,
Every hurt and teardrop God will dry.

A Year To Listen Well

1986 will mark Earth's greatest need;
Some nations shall shake like a reed.
Daniel said this generation would to
    and fro run;
They shall scream to the heavens,
    "Undone! Undone!"

Christ said, "They refused to listen
    to me."
This generation said, "Sin can set
    me free."

One World

For sure in the year of 1986
Governments shall find themselves in
    a fix.
Politicians have loudly cried that religion
    and politics cannot abide;
They have asked God and His Church to
    step aside.

When their political problems rise up to
    the sky,
And the best brains of earth cannot
    know why,
Their final answer will be to believe a lie
As Antichrist exalts himself to the sky.

1

I PREDICT FOR 1986

**I PREDICT:
THAT MILLIONS ON PLANET
EARTH WILL NOT UNDERSTAND
THIS BOOK**

I have an edict and commission from God to my generation. During this dispensation of time, planet Earth is entering its final convulsive stage of activities, both positive and negative.

All the signs of Christ's return to Earth are gathering from the colorful clouds of the western horizon. Nevertheless, as Jesus said in Matthew 16, many shall not understand.

> The Pharisees also with the Sadducees came, and tempting desired him that he would shew them a sign from heaven. He answered and said unto them, When it is evening, ye say, It will be fair weather: for the sky is red. And in the morning, It will be foul weather today: for the sky is red and lowering. O ye hypocrites, ye can discern the face of the sky; but can ye not discern the signs of the times? (Matthew 16:1-3).

Ironically, the wise men who lived two millennia ago could comprehend natural phenomena perfectly, yet they were unable to understand the spiritual signs of the times in which they lived. Those men were the leaders of a world religious system!

That same hypocrisy is strongly prevalent in modern society. For example, today when a celebrity in the entertainment world is dying with AIDS, friends and sympathizers raise fabulous amounts of money to try to save his natural life. But who speaks the words of the Bible, "The wages of sin is death," (Matthew 6:23)?

No one is willing to cry out, "Stop homosexuality! For men to make love to one another is an abomination to mankind which destroys the rightful and fruitful process of nature. It takes away the right of women to be the sole lovers of the male population."

Our generation is as confused about God's supernatural signs as those men to whom Jesus spoke in Matthew 16:1-3. Countless people living today do not know or believe that the signs mentioned in this book are actually true.

However, there are great numbers of people who do see this modern world as Jesus saw it, and as it really stands.

I trust these truths will reach your mind and heart.

14

I PREDICT:
A TIME OF PROPHETIC SPECULATION

When I was a youth living in Mobile, Alabama, a man in our church predicted that Jesus would come at midnight on New Year's Eve.

For the next few weeks our church people prepared for the Lord's return.

New Year's Eve, as we neared the midnight hour, the church members were present and scared.

At 11:45 p.m. the man stood up and in a loud voice declared, "God has just spoken to me that He has delayed the return of Christ." He walked out of the church and went home.

I was shocked. The church was shocked.

It was a false alarm.

Clearly, the man's prophecy was <u>speculation,</u> as the Bible teaches that no man knows the day or the hour when the Son of man cometh (Matthew 25:13).

15

Prophecy Is For Confirmation

When prophecy is used by man for
      speculation,
It loses the force, the wisdom of
      confirmation.
It was Christ who spoke of the future by
      saying,
"When signs appear, you know my will
      you are obeying."
If you use coming events just to speculate,
You will with one another have hot debate.

When Israel rose up from one hundred
      lands
And entered Palestine by divine
      command,
Prophecy was no longer a matter of
      speculation,
But it called His Church to dedication.

Christ proclaimed His return to
      planet Earth
Would be accompanied by millions
      coming to rebirth.

16

Today it is confirmed on mountain, land
and sea,
So prophecy is resplendent and fulfilled
for all to see.

I PREDICT:
THE FINAL MOVE OF EARTH'S TREASURE

Listen, my friend, to the movement of
treasure:
From Egypt, Babylon, Greece, and Rome
it moved without measure.
In the dark vaults of the nations it was hid;
Then suddenly emerged for power to bid.

The Spanish, the Portuguese, and the
French
From others did world treasure wrench.
Earth's treasure fleeted from land to land,
Leaving behind its memory in the sand.

Now, in the last times of this present
dispensation,
God will do that which baffles human
imagination.

To Jehovah's sons involved in worldwide
    Truth distribution,
Saints and sinners shall joyfully make their
    contribution.
The wealth for telling God's Truth shall
    like a wave roll;
From east to west we shall gather the gold.

The wealth shall not be used for the
    coffers of men,
But millions of immortals it shall win—
A mighty harvest of souls which shall
    be saved in a day.
Faith and finance shall be given to those
    who pray.

I PREDICT
THE WORLD MONETARY SYSTEM
WILL DEFAULT

This modern world is bankrupt and does
not seem to know it. Most of the western
world nations are in great difficulty finan-
cially because the so-called "Third World"
nations have borrowed unreasonable
amounts of money which they have no
means to repay.

18

How long this can continue, no one can determine. The best business brains of the world are searching for a remedy to this fiscal nightmare.

I predict that the world monetary system will default. The frightening chaos will occur at the time Antichrist emerges, proclaiming himself as a world political leader.

In Daniel 8:25 the Bible states,

And through his policy also he shall cause craft to prosper in his hand; and he shall magnify himself in his heart, and by peace shall destroy many: he shall also stand up against the Prince of princes; but he shall be broken without hand.

The Antichrist will cause a sinister kind of prosperity to go throughout the world. He will extol himself, according to Daniel. Furthermore, the Antichrist will challenge Jesus, the Prince of princes.

Still, the prophecy remains, "...he shall be broken..."

19

I PREDICT:
CIVILIAN REBELLION BY LITIGATION

At the time of the demise of the great Grecian Empire, the civilians of Athens were bringing lawsuits against each other until it was not possible for them to unite as an effective fighting machine.

One of the remarkable signs of the soon return of the Lord is rebellion by court procedures.

Christ Rebuked Unrighteous Attorneys

Jesus reprimanded unscrupulous lawyers,

And he said, Woe unto you also, ye lawyers! for ye lade men with burdens grievous to be borne, and ye yourselves touch not the burdens with one of your fingers. Woe unto you, lawyers! for ye have taken away the key of knowledge: ye entered not in yourselves, and them that were entering in ye hindered (Luke 11:46, 52).

20

The Apostle Paul Addressed Court Actions

In I Corinthians 6:1-3 the Apostle Paul wrote,

Dare any of you, having a matter against another, go to law before the unjust, and not before the saints? Do ye not know that the saints shall judge the world? and if the world shall be judged by you, are ye unworthy to judge the smallest matters? Know ye not that we shall judge angels? how much more things that pertain to this life?

I Predict That America Will Die In Court

Americans are being urged by the mass media to sue someone, anyone, for anything. Television advertisements boldly encourage, "Take them to court."

Doctors are afraid. Their patients, whom they lovingly help back to health, now take litigation into their hands and sue for malpractice.

21

Manufacturers are haunted with fear. The goods they create and manufacture can cause them to be taken to court.

Undoubtedly, America has legal paranoia and is headed for a social revolution. The courts are simply glutted with prosecutions.

In San Francisco there is a lawyer for every 213 citizens; New York has one for every 222 persons; Boston claims a legal consultant for every 227 residents.

Divorce And Broken Homes Are Killing America

Possibly, the most common legal action is divorce. The judges' chambers in every large city are inundated with cases.

Whereas ten years ago there were 700 counselors-at-law specializing in divorce proceedings, there are now 11,000 divorce experts.

A multibillion dollar industry, divorce is now one of America's booming businesses. There are one million, two hundred thousand divorces annually with legal fees alone reaching three billion dollars.

I PREDICT:
THE IONOSPHERE WILL HELP BRING BACK THE KING

Violent explosions on the sun, with amazing flames leaping into space for 75,000 miles, cause sun spots and affect the ionosphere, a belt which circles planet Earth.

This ion belt moves up and down from 75 miles to 250 miles above the earth. TV voices and pictures go right through the ionosphere, and AM radio penetrates it also.

The home ham radio operator discovered that his voice was going great distances. Through him the shortwave radio was born.

Today all major nations use shortwave radio for propaganda. Anywhere in America you can take a small shortwave radio, which fits into your palm, and listen to Moscow, Paris, India, and China.

By granting LeSEA permission to build and air such a station, the Federal Communications Commission enables this ministry to reach one-fourth of the total world population, or one billion, 300 million people.

Although First World countries receive the mass media of television, the Second and Third World nations are absorbed by shortwave radio. Hundreds of millions listen.

They are our target!

Multitudes have never heard the message of salvation preached by the anointing of the Holy Spirit.

THEY NOW CAN HEAR!

Matthew 24:14 records the words of Jesus, ''And this gospel of the kingdom shall be preached in all the world for a witness unto all nations; and then shall the end come.''

I predict He shall come soon. The ionosphere rebounding the shortwave signal will help bring back the King!

I PREDICT:
THE AMAZING RISE OF
FALSE PROPHETS

Our world has always had men and women who lie about coming events. We have and will have a proliferation of date setters, self-styled prophets, and self-interest entrepreneurs.

Jesus prophesied of numerous false prophets in Matthew 24:11, "And many false prophets shall rise, and shall deceive many."

As well as declaring that they were deceivers of the people, Jesus further stated in Matthew 7:15, "Beware of false prophets, which come to you in sheep's clothing, but inwardly they are ravening wolves."

John, the apostle, added a warning in I John 4:1, "Beloved, believe not every spirit, but try the spirits whether they are of God: because many false prophets are gone out into the world."

25

Also, Peter cautioned the Church in II Peter 2:1,17,

> But there were false prophets also among the people, even as there shall be false teachers among you, who privily shall bring in damnable heresies, even denying the Lord that bought them, and bring upon themselves swift destruction. These are wells without water, clouds that are carried with a tempest; to whom the mist of darkness is reserved for ever.

False prophets are wells without water and clouds without rain. They are empty and have no life in them.

You can recognize them because they always prophesy for self gain and self praise.

I PREDICT:
100 MILLION AMERICANS WILL NEED DELIVERANCE FROM SATANIC FORCES

For the second time my wife, three sons and I were living in the great capital city of Manila, Philippines, serving as pastors of that great congregation.

One day I was invited by the President to a special State of the Union address. The archbishop sat near me on my right, and the American ambassador sat nearby on my left. Dignitaries and statesmen listened to the address.

As we departed the Congress building, an angry crowd was gathered in the street. Most of its abuse was against America, not the Philippine government. With the yelling, there were also signs which read: "Go home, white monkeys!" "America is imperialist!"

Walking among the people, I reached the boy carrying the sign, "Go home, white monkeys!" I said, "Son, are you speaking to me? I am white. Am I a monkey?"

He replied, "No, sir!"

"Then why do you carry this sign?" I asked.

"Sir, I was paid to carry it. I am working."

"But, son, you'll get hurt. Throw down that sign."

27

He did, and I stomped it to pieces. Then I approached the youth carrying the sign, "America is imperialist!"

Of the young man I inquired, "Son, are you a student of history?"

"No," he replied.

"Yet your sign says, 'America is imperialist!'" I stated.

"Sir, I was paid to carry the sign. I need money."

"You may get hurt in this mob of people. You should throw it down."

He did, and I trampled it to splinters.

By this time I was weeping, for I love my country and know it is a good place to live.

My church in Manila is two blocks from the government buildings on Taft Avenue, the main artery of the city. While I sat at my desk crying over the people, God spoke to me to strengthen my spirit, "I am sending you back to America to help save your nation. It is in terrible condition."

God told me of conditions which would prevail in these last days. One of them was that there would be 100 million Americans mentally tormented and emotionally depressed. I could hardly believe what the Spirit was speaking into my heart. How could it be?

The Spirit answered, "Spiritism, Oriental cults, sex deviations, pornographic films, and lewd television programs will lead millions of Americans to demoniac aberrations."

Recently an article in the *U.S. News And World Report* stated that some 30 million Americans are now suffering mental depressions for various reasons.[1]

There could be more.

Also, a short time ago a *Time Magazine* article reported the story "The 27 Faces of Charles."[2] Psychiatrists discovered 27 distinct entities manifesting in Charles. He had at least 27 spirits activating him, and it was medical doctors who reported their existence.

God promised me that I could pray a prayer of deliverance for these, espec-

ially on television, and they would be set
FREE!

A great number of persons have writ-
ten to me, saying, "Your prayer of
deliverance has set me free, and I am so
glad."

Because I shall continue to pray for the
oppressed, I predict their deliverance.

I PREDICT:
THE DISSOLUTION OF THE
UNITED NATIONS

The United Nations is a modern-day
empire established in 1945 by the victorious allied nations of World War II.
Created to bring world peace, it has failed
miserably.

After watching its birth closely, I would
not have thought it could last 40 years.

When President Truman asked to have
prayer included in the opening ceremonies
of the United Nations, Russia insisted that
there would be no prayer offered to any
God, or they would not participate.
Therefore, the United Nations is an

organization that stated deliberately, "We represent nations without God."

The UN and its activities seldom represent justice or freedom because of the dominance of the Communist and Third World voting block. It became obedient to pressures from countries who had and still have no money. Yet while other nations pay the bills, Third World countries make decisions. The hands of the UN are tied by nations which refuse to let the name of Jesus be mentioned in any meetings.

One study of the United Nations declared that human torture was practiced by at least 98 of its member nations. Prisoners were subjected to electric shock, sexual abuse, beatings, or long periods of handcuffings. Some captives' heads were submerged in water or chemicals, and their flesh was burned with sulfuric acid. In Russia prisoners were forcibly given disorienting drugs.

Although the United Nations officially recognized Israel on November 29, 1947, it has generally revealed weakness, insecurity, indecision, and moral erosion in UN decisions regarding Jerusalem.

Jerusalem is a holy place unto God. He has made certain laws regarding this city, and if you violate them, you will be judged. Zechariah 12:9 says, "And it shall come to pass in that day, that I will seek to destroy all the nations that come against Jerusalem."

Every decision made by the United Nations has been negative regarding Jerusalem. They do not side with Jerusalem or with the people of Israel. I can see nothing but problems for this organization.

The UN is faltering at Jerusalem. How can you have peace without the Prince of Peace? Jesus will accomplish what the United Nations could not do. He is the answer to the UN.

I PREDICT:
THE QUITTERS WILL QUIT

The Apostle Paul said many would be

falling away in the last days. II Thessalonians 2:3 admonishes, "Let no man deceive you by any means: for that day shall not come, except there come a falling away first, and that man of sin be revealed, the son of perdition."

Paul warned that some individuals will abandon the true faith. I Timothy 4:1, "Now the Spirit speaketh expressly, that in the latter times some shall depart from the faith, giving heed to seducing spirits, and doctrines of devils."

Jesus asked if there would be faith found on the earth when He returns. Luke 18:8, "...Nevertheless when the Son of man cometh, shall he find faith on the earth?"

The quitters, as never before,
Shall run when the enemy makes a roar.
The quitters from high and low post,
Like a wilted flower, shall give up
    the ghost.

They will be blinded by Satan to the
    great power;
The quitters will lose the promises for
    this hour.

The quitters are preachers and laymen,
    too—
Their excuse shall be, ''I don't know
    what to do.''

The Holy Ghost cries to all who will hear,
''The total victory is now very near.''
The believers will speak with a voice
    of contentment,
And hell will shake and tremble at the
    judgment.

For at the end of the Dispensation
    of Grace,
Of sin and rebellion there will not be
    a trace.
The Holy Spirit is giving His final call;
This global ingathering shall be for all.

The Africans, Asians, and Europeans, too.
Millions will not know what to do!
So do not quit before Jesus arrives;
He has promised to return from the skies!

Notes

1. Lawrence D. Maloney, ''Take Mental Patients Off The Streets, Back To Hospitals?'' *U.S. News And World Report* 1 July 1985:55.
2. John Leo, ''The 27 Faces Of Charles,'' *Time Magazine* 25 October 1982:70.

2

I PREDICT:

THE 20-YEAR-CYCLE-OF-DEATH OF AMERICAN PRESIDENTS MUST CEASE

The 140-Year-Cycle Must Stop!

Every 20 years an American President dies in office. Is there a cycle-of-death for Presidents of the United States? For over 140 years the President voted in on the zero years succumbs during his administration.

I cannot accept this as a death cycle for American Presidents. I do not believe it is a curse or the influence of the stars, for astrology has no power over human life.

However, this 20-year periodicity has come to world attention and no doubt gives aspiring Presidents a feeling of uncertainty. It is possible to develop a paranoid schizophrenic attitude toward American Presidents regarding dying in office.

Many are asking, "What is this mathematical calculation by which every two decades a U.S. President expires during his service?" Three illustrious leaders died of natural causes; four have suffered violent deaths.

The 140 Years

(1) In 1840 General William Henry Harrison was elected the ninth President of the United States. He had been Governor of the Indiana Territory which reached from the state of Ohio to the Rocky Mountains, and he led the Battle of Tippecanoe in Indiana on November 7, 1811. Upon being elected President, he was

so enthusiastic that he died of exhaustion, exposure, and pneumonia within a month.

(2)   The Great Emancipator, Abraham Lincoln, was elected the 16th President in 1860. He led this nation through its greatest crisis, the Civil War, setting slaves free. A few days before he was shot by John Wilkes Booth at 10:13 p.m. on April 14, 1865, Lincoln dreamed of his death and saw his coffin in the East Room of the White House (reported by Ward Hill Lamon, his law partner).

(3)   The 20th President of our nation was James A. Garfield. He often preached to large audiences. Favored in 1880, this fine-featured, athletic man had been a college president and a Civil War General. He was killed by an angry job seeker, Charles Guiteau, a member of the Stalwarts who were seeking government favors. Garfield lingered 79 days after being shot while in a railroad station in Washington.

(4)   William McKinley was voted in as the 25th President in 1900. Under his leadership the U.S. annexed Hawaii and

conducted the 100 day war with Spain. Also, America received Puerto Rico, Guam, and the Philippines in a treaty.

McKinley was shot by Leon Czolzosz, a factory worker, in Buffalo, New York, while shaking hands with well wishers.

(5) Elected the 29th President of the U.S. in 1920, Warren G. Harding died of natural causes. While traveling from Alaska back to the state of Washington, he contracted food poisoning and died of pneumonia in San Francisco. During his administration, Harding dedicated the Lincoln Memorial and the Tomb of the Unknown Soldier in Arlington National Cemetery.

(6) Franklin Delano Roosevelt, the 32nd President, won his third term in 1940. He died a natural death on April 12, 1945. Though he signed the Declaration of War against Japan and Germany, President Roosevelt died in the midst of World War II.

(7) The next death in office occurred to the 35th President, John F. Kennedy. After being selected by the citizens to serve as their leader in 1960, Kennedy

was gunned down in Dallas, Texas on November 22, 1963. Possibly, President Kennedy had some premonition of his premature death. After a quarter century, controversy still surrounds his murder. The accused killer's wife wants the body of Oswald to be exhumed and reidentified. Were there two gunmen or only one?

(8) In the year 1980 Ronald Reagan was chosen as the 40th President of the United States. There was an assassination attempt on his life, but God preserved him. Since his reelection in 1984, President Reagan experienced cancer surgery in 1985.

Christians must pray for this cycle of death to be broken. Daily prayer for our President by millions of believing people can break any negative power over our nation.

The Bible says in Daniel 2:20-21,

Daniel answered and said, Blessed be the name of God for ever and ever: for wisdom and might are his: And he changeth the times and the seasons: he removeth kings, and setteth up kings: he giveth wisdom unto the wise, and knowledge to them that know understanding.

39

3

GEORGE WASHINGTON PREDICTED:

THE FUTURE OF THE WORLD AND AMERICA

George Washington, the first president of the United States, had a vision during the war with Britain (1812 to 1815). The details of the vision were communicated to Professor Totten by Anthony Sherman, who was with George Washington at Valley Forge.

It was a chilly, cloudless day. George Washington came out of his quarters after being there alone for more than thirty minutes. According to Anthony Sherman, the President looked paler than usual. He spoke to Anthony Sherman and relayed a vision in which a beautiful figure had just appeared to him. Washington felt as one who was dying. The image pointed and he saw the whole world and all the nations of the world.

The figure said, "Son of the Republic, look and learn." Later Washington himself recorded the following passage.

I do not know whether it is owing to the anxiety of my mind, or what, but this afternoon as I was sitting at this very table engaged in preparing a dispatch, something in the apartment seemed to disturb me. Looking up, I beheld standing opposite me a singularly beautiful female. So astonished was I, for I had given strict orders not to be disturbed, it was some moments before I found language to inquire the cause of her presence. A second, a third, and even a fourth time, did I repeat

41

my question, but received no answer from my mysterious visitor except a slight raising of the eyes.

By this time I felt strange sensations spreading through me. I would have risen, but the riveted gaze of the being before me rendered volition impossible. I essayed once more to address her, but my tongue had become powerless. Even thought itself suddenly became paralyzed. A new influence, mysterious, potent, irresistible, took possession of me. All I could do was to gaze steadily, vacantly, at my unknown visitant. Gradually the surrounding atmosphere seemed as though it became filled with sensations, and grew luminous. Everything about me seemed to rarefy, the mysterious visitor herself becoming airy, and yet more distinct to my sight than before. I now began to feel as one dying, or rather to experience the sensations which I have sometimes imagined accompany dissolution. I did not think, I did not reason, I did not move — all were alike impossible. I was only conscious of gazing fixedly, vacantly at my companion.

Presently I heard a voice saying, "Son of the Republic, look and learn." At the same time my visitor extended her arm eastward. I now beheld a heavy white vapor at some distance rising fold upon fold. This gradually dissipated, and I looked upon a strange scene. Before me lay Europe, Asia, Africa and America. I saw rolling and tossing between Europe and America the billows of the Atlantic, and between Asia and America lay the Pacific. At that moment I beheld a dark shadowy being like an angel standing, or floating in midair between Europe and America. Dipping water out of the ocean in the hollow of each hand, he sprinkled some upon America with his right hand, while with his left hand he cast some on Europe. Immediately a dark cloud raised from these countries and joined in mid-ocean. For awhile it remained stationary and then moved slowly westward, until it enveloped America in its murky folds. Sharp flashes of lightning gleamed through it at intervals, and I heard the groans and cries of the American people.

A second time the angel dipped water from the ocean, and sprinkled it as before. The dark cloud was then drawn back to the ocean, in whose heaving billows it sank from view.

I cast my eyes upon America and beheld villages and towns and cities springing up, one after another until the whole land from the Atlantic to the Pacific was dotted with them. Again I heard the mysterious voice say, "Son of the Republic, the end of the century cometh; look and learn."

At this the dark, shadowy angel turned his face southward, and from Africa I saw an ill-omened spectre approach our land. It flitted slowly and heavily over every town and city of the latter. The inhabitants presently set themselves in battle array against each other.

As I continued looking, a bright angel, on whose brow rested the word "Union," bearing the American flag, which he placed between the divided nation said, "Remember ye are brethren." Instantly the inhabitants, casting from them their weapons, became friends once more and united around the National Standard.

The dark, shadowy angel placed a trumpet to his mouth and blew three blasts; and taking water from the ocean, he sprinkled it upon Europe, Asia and Africa. Then my eyes beheld a fearful scene: From each of these countries arose thick black clouds that were soon joined into one. Throughout this mass there gleamed a dark red light by which I saw hordes of armed men, who moved with the cloud, marching by land and sailing by sea to America, which country was enveloped in the volume of the cloud. And I dimly saw these vast armies devastate the whole country and burn the villages, towns and cities that I had beheld springing up. As my ears listened to the thundering of the cannon, clashing of swords and shouts and cries of millions in mortal combat, I again heard the mysterious voice saying, "Son of the Republic, look and learn."

When the voice had ceased, the dark, shadowy angel placed his trumpet once more to his mouth and blew a loud and fearful blast.

Instantly a light as of a thousand suns shone down from above me and broke into fragments the dark cloud which enveloped America. At the same moment the angel upon whose head still shone the word "Union," and who bore our national flag in one hand and a sword in the other, descended from heaven attended by legions of bright spirits. These immediately joined the inhabitants of America, who, I perceived, were well nigh overcome, but who, immediately taking courage again, closed up their broken ranks and renewed the battle.

Again amid the fearful noise of the conflict, I heard the mysterious voice saying, "Son of the Republic, look and learn."

As the voice ceased, the shadowy angel for the last time dipped water from the ocean and sprinkled it upon America. Instantly the dark cloud rolled back, together with the armies it had brought, leaving the inhabitants of the land victorious...

The first President of the United States, like the prophet Daniel, was given a vision of the destiny of his nation.

I Daniel was grieved in my spirit in the midst
of my body, and the visions of my head troubled
me. I came near unto one of them that stood
by, and asked him the truth of all this. So he
told me, and made me know the interpretation
of the things (Daniel 7:15-16).

4

I PREDICT:

SIGNS OF THE
LAST DAYS

Just before the return of our Lord, there will be divine intervention into the affairs of men.

Domestic Intervention

I cannot forget a case where God clearly intervened in a household.

One Sunday I was attending church when a neighbor woman walked into the service. At the invitation for salvation, she came forward to receive Christ as her Savior.

While she was yet praying, her alcoholic husband entered the building in a terrible rage. Cursing with every step, he rushed down the middle aisle of the church. He literally picked up his wife in his arms and roughly proceeded to carry her out of the church.

Immediately the pastor sought to intercede and talk with the man. Mr. Morris was a big bulk of a man and raised his fist to the pastor, threatening to strike him if he interfered.

As the man stalked out of the building, we could hear his wife weeping and asking forgiveness while her husband continued to blaspheme God. The pastor called the entire congregation to prayer for that family. It was certainly a dramatic moment to witness.

The next afternoon at 3:30 a terrible thunderstorm hit the area. One of the power lines broke and fell across the street from the church.

This same man, who caused so much commotion in the church the night before, worked for the electric company. He was called to assist with the repairs on the power line that was down.

I stood by the church and watched his big rubber boots slip on an exposed iron water pipe. As he fell to the ground, a live high tension wire dropped across his body. Within seconds he was dead, although fellow workmen tried every available means to save his life.

Not 50 steps from where he had cursed God the night before, he died. Everyone who attended that meeting realized that God does intervene in the affairs of men.

Divine Intervention In Nations

From the beginning of history God has evaluated nations. Genesis 12:3, ''And I will bless them that bless thee, and curse him that curseth thee: and in thee shall all families of the earth be blessed.''

Babylon was earmarked for destruction,

and it was God's own hand that wrote the verdict on the wall of Belshazzar's banquet hall.

Daniel 5:5 describes the scene.

> In the same hour came forth fingers of a man's hand, and wrote over against the candlestick upon the plaster of the wall of the king's palace: and the king saw the part of the hand that wrote.''

God is also prophesying to modern nations.

No doubt Russia is a marked nation. Ezekiel 38 and 39 tell exactly what Russia will do. She is preparing for it at this moment by arming Near East and African countries for an overland invasion toward Israel.

The Book of The Revelation announces that the kings of the East will march to Armageddon.

> And the sixth angel poured out his vile upon the great river Euphrates; and the water thereof was dried up, that the way of the kings of the east might be prepared (Revelation 16:12).

Japan, China, and India are preparing themselves for a great final showdown with God. Their religions of Hinduism, Buddhism, Shintoism, and Confucianism must be judged before God.

Divine Intervention In Religion

There are denominations and churches which God has selected for judgment. In the third chapter of Revelation God spoke of the Laodicean church and declared He would spew it out of His mouth because of its lukewarmness.

Certainly, God will visit in judgment the churches of America that have denied the virgin birth, that have refused miracles, and that have declared the Gifts of the Spirit obsolete.

Divine Intervention In Morals

God holds the judicial system and the clergy responsible for the morals of the people. When they fail to warn the nation or to judge iniquity, then God intervenes.

Adultery is wrong, and when those responsible to judge were derelict in their duties, the plagues of gonorrhea and syphilis came. These afflictions rendered some men sterile, and produced diseased children by others.

When homosexuals and lesbians rose up to challenge the normal home, and the judicial system with the support of the clergy refused to act in the fear of God, then God judged with AIDS and put an entire country in a state of panic. AIDS is a dark cloud over all life.

1986 will be a year of God revealing His power to judge planet Earth. Leviticus 26:18-19 warn,

> And if ye will not yet for all this hearken unto me, then I will punish you seven times more for your sins. And I will break the pride of your power; and I will make your heaven as iron, and your earth as brass.

Some people are headed for Antichrist and the Great Tribulation. Others are indicated for the Rapture of the Church.

How are you marked?

You must decide now!

5

I PREDICT:

THE FULFILLMENT OF TWO GREAT SIGNS SPOKEN BY JESUS CHRIST

The Sign Of Noah

Matthew 24:37-39 describes the sign of Noah.

But as the days of Noe were, so shall also the coming of the Son of man be. For as in the days that were before the flood they were eating and drinking, marrying and giving in marriage, until the day that Noe entered into the ark, and knew not until the flood came, and took them all away; so shall also the coming of the Son of man be.

The man Noah witnessed an amazing disintegration of normal, moral society. Watching the family system falter, he observed husbands, wives, and children suffering trauma in their total emotional persons.

Noah comforted broken hearts and sought to reunite devastated homes. At the same time he strengthened his own household by keeping it spiritually oriented.

Genesis 6:8 records, ''But Noah found grace in the eyes of the Lord.'' God said that this man stood out as a unique figure in his time.

Because Noah believed what God said, he built an ark to rescue his family. Hebrews 11:7 testifies,

By faith Noah, being warned of God of things not seen as yet, moved with fear, prepared an ark to the saving of his house; by the which he condemned the world, and became heir of the righteousness which is by faith.

55

Eating And Drinking

There is no greater sign of the return of Christ than eating and drinking.

Today the average American consumes 1,426 pounds of food a year. This is 45 pounds more than the average American ate just 20 years ago.

Noah spoke to a gluttonous generation at the time of the flood, and Jesus prophesied of one at the time of His return.

This prophecy given by Jesus Christ is being fulfilled today.

Jesus Referred To Lot's Day

At the time of the return of Christ to earth, there will be an awful repetition of society as it was in Lot's day. Luke 17:28-30 affirms:

Likewise also as it was in the days of Lot; they did eat, they drank, they bought, they sold, they planted, they builded; But the same day that Lot went out of Sodom it rained fire and brimstone from heaven, and destroyed them all. Even thus shall it be in the day when the Son of man is revealed.

The Sign Of Lot

Lot was a man of fortune and misfortune.

He was a person of misfortune because his father, Haran, died a premature death.

However, Lot was a person of good fortune in that he had a godly uncle, named Abraham, who adopted him and permitted him to live like a son in his household.

With his blessed and prosperous Uncle Abraham, Lot shared the riches of cattle, gold, and tents.

One day ambitious Lot left his uncle's home and leadership to live in the exciting city of Sodom.

Sodom was renowned as a licentious city practicing illicit sex. After 3000 years the city-state of Sodom still bears the stigma of sodomy.

In this infamous city Lot, who had lived under the shadow of the great man of faith, observed his family crumble before his eyes. His daughters married Sodomites, and his wife was in love with Sodomic society.

He witnessed the awful judgment of

57

Jehovah against the willful wickedness of Sodom and its sister city, Gomorrah. As the fire rained down from heaven, Lot and his two single daughters were the only escapees.

Today mankind is trying to convince itself that deviate sexual behavior is normal. Three thousand years of history prove it is wrong. The scourge of syphilis and AIDS support the scripture which says, ''the wages of sin is death'' (Romans 6:23).

If all the roosters were like the gays, there would be no eggs on the table. If all the hogs became homosexual, there would be no more bacon. If all the bulls were perverted, there would be no steaks. If all the men were sodomites, this would be earth's last generation.

This social aberration is a sign Jesus gave of the time of His return.

6

I PREDICT:

THE GREATEST PERSON OF PROPHECY WILL SOON RETURN TO PLANET EARTH

Hundreds of years before Jesus was born the prophets spoke of His birthplace.

But thou, Bethlehem Ephratah, though thou be little among the thousands of Judah, yet out of thee shall he come forth unto me that is to be ruler in Israel; whose goings forth have been from of old, from everlasting (Micah 5:2).

The great prophet Isaiah prophesied the nature and ministry of Jesus.

For he shall grow up before him as a tender plant, and as a root out of a dry ground: he hath no form nor comeliness; and when we shall see him, there is no beauty that we should desire him. He is despised and rejected of men; a man of sorrows, and acquainted with grief: and we hid as it were our faces from him; he was despised, and we esteemed him not. Surely he hath borne our griefs, and carried our sorrows: yet we did esteem him stricken, smitten of God, and afflicted. But he was wounded for our transgressions, he was bruised for our iniquities: the chastisement of our peace was upon him; and with his stripes we are healed. (Isaiah 53:2-5).

Jesus responded to this tremendous prophecy in Luke 4:18.

The Spirit of the Lord is upon me, because he hath anointed me to preach the gospel to the poor; he hath sent me to heal the brokenhearted, to preach deliverance to the captives, and recovering of sight to the blind, to set at liberty them that are bruised.

A vibrant, challenging spiritual leader, Jesus prophesied of His own death.

Saying, The Son of man must suffer many things, and be rejected of the elders and chief priests and scribes, and be slain, and be raised the third day (Luke 9:22).

The greatest prophetic event of the future is Christ's return. Angels said He will return in the same manner in which He left. Acts 1:10-11 record the signs of His return.

And while they looked stedfastly toward heaven as he went up, behold, two men stood by them in white apparel; which also said, Ye men of Galilee, why stand ye gazing up into heaven? this same Jesus, which is taken up from you into heaven, shall so come in like manner as ye have seen him go into heaven.

I predict the soon return to planet Earth of the most prophetic person of all history.

7

I PREDICT:

THE MOST INCREDULOUS MIRACLE OF DIVINE INTERVENTION INTO HUMAN AFFAIRS TO BE IMMINENT

Our generation will experience the most challenging move of God that mankind has ever known: the greatest demonstration in history of all nine Gifts of the Holy Spirit, as recorded in I Corinthians chapter 12.

Miracles will be released in a glory not yet known to man. Millions will rejoice at divine interventions into human affairs.

Dr. Charles Price

In my young ministry one of the greatest evangelists that I met was Dr. Charles S. Price. He was conducting a large tent crusade in Pomona, California. I knew about him because I had studied his magazine, *The Golden Grain,* and greatly admired his exposition of God's Word.

Charles Price was a prince of preachers and possessed a tremendous anointing to pray for the sick.

Before he went to heaven, he told Howard Carter, a personal friend of mine, that God had given him a vision of inconceivable miracles of divine intervention into human affairs. In this vision he saw the dead raised, the crippled healed, and vast numbers of people rejoicing in the living God.

With a rush of tears from his eyes, he said, "Howard, we shall not live to see this, but our coming generation will see it."

I am that generation, and I predict its fulfillment!

Smith Wigglesworth

One of the most renowned ministers of the 20th century was Smith Wigglesworth of England. He challenged, and sometimes frightened, whole nations. His meetings in Norway, Sweden, Denmark, Switzerland, South Africa, Australia, and United States were phenomena of Holy Spirit miracles.

I was very close to Smith Wigglesworth in his last years. Although he was in his 80s and I was in my 20s, I was as eager as Timothy to learn, and he was as magnanimous as the Apostle Paul to teach.

Toward the end of our keen fellowship together, he embraced me one day in his home and said, ''Young man, I see it. I see it.''

With tears flowing he said, ''It's unbelievable.''

God will pour out signs and wonders all over this earth which will cause hosts of humans to come to Christ. No one will be able to count the mighty miracles of God. Some will be judgment miracles against those who resist God and revile His works.

Most will be healing miracles with the impossible becoming possible and the incredible becoming a reality.

Smith Wigglesworth said, "Young man, I cannot live to see this, but you will see it, and I place all of the faith within my bosom upon you to go forth and live in the holy anointing of God."

I predict the most incredulous miracle of divine intervention in human affairs in all of history. Prepare yourself for this thrilling move of the Most High God.

Other books by Lester Sumrall:

LeSEA Publishing Co.
- Conscience—The Scales Of Eternal Justice
- Dominion Is Yours
- Genesis—Crucible Of The Universe
- Imagination
- Joseph—Trajectory Of Faith
- Paul—Man Of The Millennia
- The Will—The Potent Force Of The Universe
- The Battle Of The Ages
- The Total Man
- The Human Soul
- The Human Body
- The Human Spirit

Nelson Publishing Co.
- Demons The Answer Book
- Grief—You Can Conquer It
- Hostility
- Jerusalem, Where Empires Die—
  Will America Die At Jerusalem?
- Making Life Count
- My Story To His Glory
- 60 Things God Said About Sex
- Supernatural Principalities & Powers
- The Names Of God
- The Reality Of Angels
- Where Was God When Pagan
  Religions Began?

Harrison House
- Faith To Change The World
- Gifts & Ministries Of The Holy Spirit
- Jihad—The Holy War
- Unprovoked Murder
- Victory & Dominion Over Fear
- 101 Questions & Answers On Demon Power